|  | Date: |  |
| | Version #: 1.0 | C000155766 |

Confidential

CYBER SECURITY
RESOURCE

Threat and Vulnerability Management Guide

Table of Contents

Introduction

For a downloadable word document go to https://cybersecurityresource.com/portfolio/vulnerability-management-program/ and select "Access Tools and Templates" and use coupon code **Vuln57** at check out.

Purpose

The main objective of the Threat and Vulnerability Management (TVM) Program is to establish and maintain plans, procedures, and technologies to detect, identify, analyze, manage, and respond to cybersecurity threats and vulnerabilities.

NIST defines a vulnerability as being a "Weakness in an information system, system security procedures, internal controls, or implementation that could be exploited or triggered by a threat source."

There are several reasons organizations should implement a robust TVM Program:

- Most importantly, a robust TVM Program is very effective in helping organizations mitigate the risk of a cybersecurity breach.
- It is required by law as set forth in the Health Insurance Portability and Accountability Act (HIPAA) of.
- It is policy.

    - COMPANY Policy, Minimum Security Standards for Network Devices, revised August 31, 2012, defines required technical standards and minimum configuration for all workstations, servers, and networking equipment connected to COMPANY Health Sciences networks. A robust TVM Program is essential to support and enforce this policy.

Only by identifying and remediating threats and vulnerabilities inherent in the enterprise architecture can attackers be prevented from penetrating networks and accessing Restricted Information such as electronic protected health information (ePHI). A structured and disciplined approach to discovering and remediating, or mitigating, threats and vulnerabilities is necessary to prevent information exploitation and theft.

The TVM Program, as prescribed, consists of three major activities (Fig. 1):

- Program Governance – Defines the program charter, mission, and mandate; describes roles and responsibilities required to execute threat and vulnerability management processes effectively; and provides for necessary oversight and reporting requirements.
- Threat Management – Defines managing emerging threats and preventive measures an organization can take to address potential threats and risks proactively.
- Vulnerability Management – Defines managing vulnerabilities once they are identified as well as responsive measures that an organization can take to help ensure they are prioritizing and remediating, or isolating, known vulnerabilities.

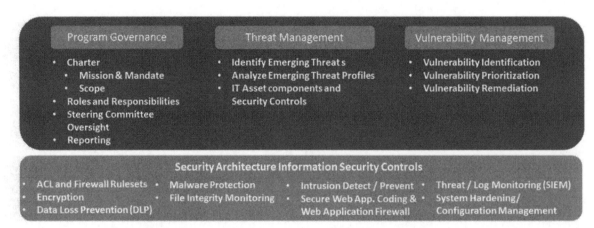

Figure 1. Threat and Vulnerability Management Program Structure

Background

The intent of this document is to create organized and repeatable threat and vulnerability management processes to enhance the overall security posture of COMPANY Health Sciences networks, systems, and applications as well as providing better protection for Restricted Information.

This document was created utilizing industry accepted best practices from the following organizations:

- Center for Internet Security (CIS)
- Information Systems Audit and Control Association (ISACA)
- International Organization for Standardization (ISO)/International Electrotechnical Commission (IEC)
- System Administration, Audit, Network, and Security (SANS) Institute
- U.S. Department of Commerce, National Institute of Standards and Technology (NIST)
- U.S. Department of Energy, Office of Electricity Delivery and Energy Reliability

The security controls included in this document have been adapted from documents listed in Appendix A and are essential for a mature TVM Program. Some controls are applicable only to the TVM Program and should be controlled directly from within the Program while other controls are supporting controls not under the direct control or responsibility of the TVM Program.

Continuous Vulnerability Assessment and Remediation

CIS maintains a list of Critical Security Controls for Effective Cyber Defense (i.e., the Controls). Control Number Four on the list is "Continuous Vulnerability Assessment and Remediation." This critical security control is the heart of the TVM Program because the ultimate objective is to mature the Program to the point where vulnerability assessment and remediation can be done on a continuous basis.

The steps to implement Control Number Four are listed in Table 1 below. However, before reviewing Table 1, some background information is needed on the TVM Program security control numbering format as well as the model used to assess the maturity level of COMPANY activities, controls, and processes.

TVM Program Control Number Format

Before referencing TVM Program security controls, some background information is needed on the control numbering format.

Security controls will be numbered using the format TVM-IS-Cnn, where TVM indicates the control is part of the TVM Program, IS indicates the control is within the purview of the Information Services and Solutions (IS) Department, and CNN indicates a sequential control number beginning with 01.

The IS Security Team will be responsible for developing, implementing, and monitoring the continued effectiveness of TVM Program security controls.

Maturity Indicator Level (MIL)

Elements of the Cybersecurity Capability Maturity Model (C2M2) developed by the U.S. Department of Energy, Office of Electricity Delivery and Energy Reliability, will be used throughout the TVM Program to assess the maturity of activities, controls, and processes pertaining to the deployment and implementation of security controls. The C2M2 defines four Maturity Indicator Levels (MILs) that are numbered MIL0 through MIL3 (See Figure 2).

TVM Program controls have been mapped to the steps for implementing continuous vulnerability assessment and remediation in Table 1 below. A MIL is provided that shows the difference between security controls performed by different IT organizations based on varying levels of maturity.

The ultimate objective is to achieve MIL3; however, it must be understood that will take time and effort as it does with anything to mature. As stated in a Gartner paper, "Security processes, unlike appliances, software and services, cannot be acquired in exchange for cash. They can only be established by an organization and then mature to an appropriate level."

COMPANY should establish realistic goals for achieving successively higher maturity levels. It may not be realistic to become MIL3 in the next few months, but not having a plan or waiting too long should not be acceptable to the organization either.

MIL0		
MIL1	a.	The organization has a cybersecurity program strategy
MIL2	b.	The cybersecurity program strategy defines objectives for the organization's cybersecurity activities
	c.	The cybersecurity program strategy and priorities are documented and aligned with the organization's strategic objectives and risk to critical infrastructure
	d.	The cybersecurity program strategy defines the organization's approach to provide program oversight and governance for cybersecurity activities
	e.	The cybersecurity program strategy defines the structure and organization of the cybersecurity program
	f.	The cybersecurity program strategy is approved by senior management
MIL3	g.	The cybersecurity program strategy is updated to reflect business changes, changes in the operating environment, and changes in the threat profile (TVM-1d)

Figure 2. Maturity Indicator Levels Defined in C2M2

Implementing Continuous Vulnerability Assessment and Remediation

The steps for implementing continuous vulnerability assessment and remediation along with the corresponding TVM Program control, where applicable, and the COMPANY MIL for that step/control are listed in Table 1 below.

Table 1. Steps for Continuous Vulnerability Assessment and Remediation

CSC 4 Step #/ TVM Control #	Critical Security Control Number Four Description	MIL
CSC 4-1 **TVM-IS-C02**	Run automated vulnerability scanning tools against all systems and devices on the network on a quarterly or more frequent basis and deliver prioritized lists of the most critical vulnerabilities to IT Operations along with risk scores that compare the effectiveness of efforts to reduce overall risk to COMPANY networks. Use a SCAP-validated vulnerability scanner that looks for both code-based vulnerabilities (such as those described by Common Vulnerabilities and Exposures entries) and configuration-based vulnerabilities (as enumerated by the Common Configuration Enumeration Project).	MIL 1
CSC 4-2	Correlate event logs with information from vulnerability scans to fulfill two goals. First, personnel should verify that the activity of the regular vulnerability scanning tools themselves is logged. Second, personnel should be able to correlate attack detection events with earlier vulnerability scanning results to determine whether the given exploit was used against a target known to be vulnerable. (Recommended Control: SIEM implementation)	MIL 0

Threat and Vulnerability Management Program

CSC 4 Step #/ TVM Control #	Critical Security Control Number Four Description	MIL
CSC 4-3 TVM-IS-C02	Perform vulnerability scanning in authenticated mode either with agents running locally on each end system to analyze the security configuration or with remote scanners that are given administrative rights on the system being tested. Use a dedicated account for authenticated vulnerability scans, which should not be used for any other administrative activities and should be tied to specific machines at specific IP addresses. Ensure that only authorized employees have access to the vulnerability management user interface and that roles are applied to each user.	MIL 1
CSC 4-4 TVM-IS-C01	Subscribe to vulnerability alerting services in order to stay aware of emerging exposures, and use the information gained from the alerts to update the organization's vulnerability scanning activities on an as needed basis. Alternatively, ensure vulnerability scanning tools being used are regularly updated with the most current security vulnerability information.	MIL 1
CSC 4-5 Patch Mgmt. Runbook	Deploy automated patch management tools and software update tools for operating system and software/applications on all systems for which such tools are available and safe. Patches should be applied to all systems, even systems that are properly air gapped.	MIL 1
CSC 4-6	Carefully monitor logs associated with any scanning activity and associated administrator accounts to ensure that all scanning activity and associated access via the privileged account is limited to the timeframes of legitimate scans. (Recommended Control: SIEM implementation)	MIL 0
CSC 4-7 TVM-IS-C05	Compare the results from back-to-back vulnerability scans to verify that vulnerabilities were addressed either by patching, implementing a compensating control, or documenting and accepting a reasonable business risk. Such acceptance of business risks for existing vulnerabilities should be periodically reviewed to determine if newer compensating controls or subsequent patches can address vulnerabilities that were previously accepted, or if conditions have changed, increasing the risk.	MIL 1
CSC 4-8 Patch Mgmt. Runbook	Measure the delay in patching new vulnerabilities and ensure that the delay is equal to or less than the benchmarks set forth by the organization. Alternative countermeasures should be considered if patches are not available.	MIL 1
CSC 4-9 Patch Mgmt. Runbook	Evaluate critical patches in a test environment before pushing them into production on enterprise systems. If such patches break critical business applications on test machines, the organization must devise other mitigating controls that block exploitation on systems where the patch cannot be deployed because of its impact on business functionality.	MIL 1

CSC 4 Step #/ TVM Control #	Critical Security Control Number Four Description	MIL
CSC 4-10 TVM-IS-C04 Patch Mgmt. Runbook	Establish a process to risk-rate vulnerabilities based on the exploitability and potential impact of the vulnerability, and segmented by appropriate groups of assets (example, DMZ servers, internal network servers, desktops, laptops). Apply patches for the riskiest vulnerabilities first. A phased rollout can be used to minimize the impact to the organization. Establish expected patching timelines based on the risk rating level.	MIL 1

TVM Program controls should be augmented through the implementation and maintenance of security architecture controls. Many IT security professionals consider these controls fundamental to any network security program. The controls, control description, and frequency the controls should be employed are listed in Table 2 below and are covered in more detail throughout the remainder of the TVM Program document. These controls are also included as Security Architecture Information Security Controls supporting Program Governance, Threat Management, and Vulnerability Management in Figure 1 above.

Table 2. Fundamental Security Architecture Controls

Security Architecture Control	Description	Desired Frequency
ACL & Firewall Rules	Ensuring access control lists and firewall rules are accurate, documented appropriately, and periodically reviewed.	Quarterly
Encryption	Protecting Restricted Information at rest and in motion.	Pervasive
Data Loss Prevention (Recommended)	Deploying solution to identify where Restricted Information exists on the network and to prevent the information from leaving the network.	Project
Malware Protection	Maintaining anti-virus and malware software.	Pervasive
File Integrity Monitoring	Maintaining integrity of key files, folders, and Windows Registry key/value pairs and generating alerts if changes are detected.	Pervasive
Intrusion Detection/ Prevention (IDS/IPS)	Monitoring network traffic to detect and/or prevent potential attacks and report suspicious activity.	Pervasive
Secure Web Application Coding and Web-Application Firewalls	Applying secure software development lifecycle processes and/or deploying Web Application Firewalls.	Pervasive
Threat/Log Monitoring (Recommended)	Deploying Security Information and Event Management (SIEM)-based log monitoring solution to detect potential security events.	Project

Security Architecture Control	Description	Desired Frequency
System Hardening and Configuration Management	Techniques to securely configure assets with standard configuration images.	Continuous

Program Governance

Charter

This document is intended for departments, managers, and individuals responsible for managing and implementing threat and vulnerability management processes.

The following functional requirements for the COMPANY TVM Program have been included to help ensure the needs of compliance and other regulatory bodies have been satisfied:

- Enable clear and consistent management of system wide security issues on COMPANY networks
- Enable a model for defining, communicating, and making decisions about security issues on COMPANY networks
- Create a uniform mechanism to escalate security issues and concerns to management
- Enable system wide metrics and a reporting system for vulnerability status across COMPANY networks
- Ensure Restricted Information, for which COMPANY is responsible, is adequately identified and vulnerabilities are remediated or mitigated in a timely manner or any residual risk is formally accepted.

Mission and Mandate

The mission and mandate of the TVM Program is to support the overall COMPANY Security Program strategy to enhance the security of Restricted Information on COMPANY networks. A solid framework will be established from which consistent guidance and standard operating procedures will be provided along with structured, well-defined, and repeatable processes that consistently result in the security of Restricted Information on COMPANY networks and are sufficient to meet mandated compliance requirements.

The TVM Program will have a clear reporting structure as well as guidance and support from the Security Committee (SC), defined in a subsequent section.

This document will be reviewed and refined on an as needed basis to ensure the contents remain relevant.

Scope

Implement threat and vulnerability management processes as may be required to protect Restricted Information on essential systems.

COMPANY consists of:

- COMPANY Health System (includes Hospitals and Facility Practice Group)

TVM Program effectiveness is based on the assumption an IT asset inventory has been created and is updated as new inventory is added and old inventory is retired.

The bottom line for any security program is to protect the organization's information. For the purposes of this document, we will focus on ePHI because that provides an acceptable lowest common denominator for the information that needs to be protected to comply with the HIPAA Security Rule.

The majority of the Restricted Information on COMPANY networks is ePHI but other types of Restricted Information may be included. The HIPAA Security Rule is the governing statute that mandates protection of ePHI. This statute further mandates covered entities conduct assessments of potential risks and vulnerabilities to systems containing ePHI data, and implement security measures sufficient to reduce risks and vulnerabilities to that data.

The scope of the TVM Program will not include physical security, identity and access management or security awareness; however, they may be mentioned as examples throughout this document.

Roles and Responsibilities

The roles and responsibilities of offices, teams, and/or individuals required to perform various actions in support of the TVM Program are listed below:

Office of Compliance Services (OCS)

OCS is responsible for ensuring information security controls meet various privacy, security and legal regulations, and guidelines. OCS resources are employed to review security vulnerability risk remediation and mitigation results and will work with the IS Security Team to make the final determination on whether vulnerability risk remediation or mitigation is satisfactory.

Director of IS Security

The Director of IS Security will be responsible for overseeing project completion and will serve as the central point of contact for any Issue(s) and/or escalations with sponsors, vendors, OCS, or security. This role will be responsible to help ensure that IS Security programs are being executed according to the mission and mandate of the respective programs.

IS Security Team

The IS Security Team works within the IS Department at COMPANY. The IS Security Team will be responsible for the TVM Program and for communicating the status of vulnerability remediation and mitigation. This team will include vulnerability analyst subject matter experts (SMEs) who will oversee security vulnerability processes and will provide recommendations to OCS personnel based on the results of remediation or mitigation actions. The SMEs will have direct and continuous communication with system administrators, IT Managers, and OCS.

Business Associates and Vendors (BAs/Vendors)

The IS Security Team will engage the services of various Business Associates and Vendors for specific services related to the TVM Program.

IT Operations Team (includes all IT Support Groups)

Individuals in IT that support key network security architecture controls such as Patch Management, System Hardening, and IT Asset Management.

Oversight

The Security Committee (SC) will provide oversight to the TVM Program.

Security Committee (SC)

The HSSC is responsible for providing resources to implement the TVM Program. The HSSC provides oversight to ensure high-level administrative activities are executed with the required frequency and within appropriate timelines. The HSSC reports to the Enterprise Compliance Oversight Board (ECOB) and serves as a point of escalation to the HSECOB for final decisions.

Reporting

Vulnerability statistics will be provided to the HSSC and Program Sponsors on an as needed basis. These reports should provide relevant information pertaining to identified vulnerabilities, remediated or mitigated vulnerabilities, and newly detected threats. These reports should give management the ability to make informed and expedient decisions regarding the overall security program. Additionally, a benchmark should be established from the onset of the TVM Program to allow management to see how the security posture of COMPANY networks is improving as a result of the controls and processes implemented through the TVM Program.

Maturity Levels of Program Governance Activities

As Program Governance activities mature, the level at which the activities are performed will evolve. Figure 3 below shows the governance activities performed in different IT organizations at varying maturity levels.

• No Practice at MIL 1	• Documented practices are followed for threat and vulnerability management activities	• Threat and vulnerability management activities are guided by documented policies or other organizational directives
	• Stakeholders for threat and vulnerability management activities are identified and involved	• Threat and vulnerability management policies include compliance requirements for specified standards and/or guidelines
	• Adequate resources (people, funding, and tools) are provided to support threat and vulnerability management activities	• Threat and vulnerability management activities are periodically reviewed to ensure conformance with policy
	• Standards and/or guidelines have been identified to inform threat and vulnerability management activities	• Responsibility and authority for the performance of threat and vulnerability management activities are assigned to personnel
		• Personnel performing threat and vulnerability management activities have the skills and knowledge needed to perform their assigned responsibilities
MIL 1	MIL 2	MIL 3

Figure 3. Maturity Levels of Program Governance Activities

IT Asset Management

IT Asset Management (ITAM) is important to the delivery of key business processes and is an essential activity in managing overall risk to COMPANY networks. Recording important details about assets such as type, IP address, physical location, and owner will enable many other critical security controls to function more effectively. Effective ITAM is an essential component of every TVM Program. Typically, ITAM is most often not owned by the information security department; however, this activity is being included at the beginning of this document because the fundamental importance of ITAM to the success of the TVM Program cannot be overstated. There are also elements of ITAM that do not rely on information security activities yet remain relevant to the TVM Program. Those elements will be further described in this section.

Before anything can be protected, that which needs protection must be known. Therefore, maintaining an accurate asset inventory is essential to an organization's ability to assess the organization's threat profile, perform patch management activities, conduct penetration testing, respond to zero-day exploits, and many other critical information security functions.

Before the risk assessment is performed, an inventory of all IT resources contained within the new system should be created and added to the asset inventory management system and entered into the change management system. The asset inventory should be updated on an ongoing basis as part of ongoing configuration management and patch management processes. Maintaining an accurate asset inventory will not

only facilitate several information security initiatives, it will also provide the added benefit of facilitating strategic inventory planning and preparation of procurement forecasts.

Identify Essential Systems

Not all systems are of equal importance. For example, systems that support the university's financials or key revenue generating applications are clearly more important than the server being used to store this TVM Program document. Compiling a list of essential systems to help those responsible for managing threats and vulnerabilities prioritize management strategies is a highly important exercise.

Risk assessments should identify the resource availability requirements according to the criticality and priority status of the information resources. All resources should be classified into one of the following categories:

- Essential to the continuing operation of the organization. Failure to function correctly and on schedule could result in a major failure to perform mission-critical functions, a significant loss of funds or information, or a significant liability or other legal exposure.
- Necessary to perform important functions. Operations could continue for a short period of time without those functions while normal operations are being restored.
- Deferrable for an extended period of time. Operations can continue without those systems or services performing correctly or on schedule.

An added benefit of identifying essential systems is that it provides the IS Security Team with enhanced visibility across COMPANY networks, which facilitates quick reaction to potential threats such as zero-day exploits and/or vulnerabilities which might be critical. If news of a critical vulnerability that impacts any essential systems is released, the affected systems could be easily identified and patched to remediate the vulnerabilities as quickly as possible, much like implementing an emergency change.

Identify Restricted Information

Systems containing Restricted Information have additional security requirements. The HIPAA Security Rule requires protection of information about an individual's health, referred to as electronic protected health information, or ePHI. Accordingly, specific requirements have been established for the disclosure or release of this information as well as information or records defined as public information. Unauthorized disclosure, modification, or destruction of this information could have a very adverse effect, with widespread impact to COMPANY networks and individual's privacy.

Change Management

Change management systems are designed to document changes made to a network or changes made to systems connected to networks. The well-defined and highly structured policies and procedures that exist to document changes should be utilized anytime new systems (e.g., hardware, firmware, and software) are added to any COMPANY networks. Any additions, changes, updates, or deletions of hardware or software must be captured in the change management system. Vulnerability remediation and mitigation along with patch management activities should also be well documented in the change management system.

Maturity Levels of IT Asset Management Activities

As ITAM activities become more mature, the level to which they are performed will evolve. Figure 4 below shows ITAM activities performed in different organizations at varying maturity levels.

MIL 1	MIL 2	MIL 3
• There is an inventory of OT and IT assets that are important to the delivery of the function • There is an inventory of information assets that are important to the delivery of the function (e.g., PHI, PII, financial data) • Configuration baselines are established for inventoried assets where it is desirable to ensure that multiple assets are configured similarly • Configuration baselines are used to configure assets at deployment	• Inventory attributes include information to support the cybersecurity strategy (e.g., location, asset owner, applicable security requirements, service dependencies, service level agreements, and conformance of assets to relevant industry standards) • Inventoried assets are prioritized based on their importance to the delivery of the function • The design of configuration baselines includes cybersecurity objectives	• There is an inventory for all connected IT and OT assets related to the delivery of the function • The asset inventory is current (as defined by the organization) • Configuration of assets are monitored for consistency with baselines throughout the assets' life cycle • Configuration baselines are reviewed and updated at an organizationally-defined frequency

Figure 4. Maturity Levels of ITAM Activities

Threat Management

Threat management is a critical process, or collection of processes, for identifying emerging threats to an information system along with developing and analyzing emerging threat profiles.

The SANS Institute is a sponsor of the Critical Security Controls for Effective Cyber Defense (the Controls) currently maintained by the Center for Internet Security (CIS). Control number four on the list is "Continuous Vulnerability Assessment and Remediation". At the root of this control, the SANS Institute describes the need for an organization to "Continuously acquire, assess, and take action on new information in order to identify vulnerabilities, as well as remediate, and minimize the window of opportunity for attackers." One of the more important steps in taking action on new information is staying current on emerging threats, zero-day attacks, and newly identified vulnerabilities, as well as designing controls to detect potential exploits for which no remediation exists.

The individuals identified for the roles previously discussed in the Program Governance section must always be operating in what the SANS Institute describes as "a constant stream of new information." This includes daily updates for software patches, security advisories, threat bulletins, Internet security reports, etc. These sources of threat information must be continuously monitored. Organizations that do not identify emerging threats or proactively search for new information pertaining to potential vulnerabilities run the increased likelihood of having their systems and sensitive information compromised.

Identify Emerging Threats Process Flow Diagram

The process flow for identifying emerging threats is illustrated in the Swim Lane Diagram in Figure 5 below.

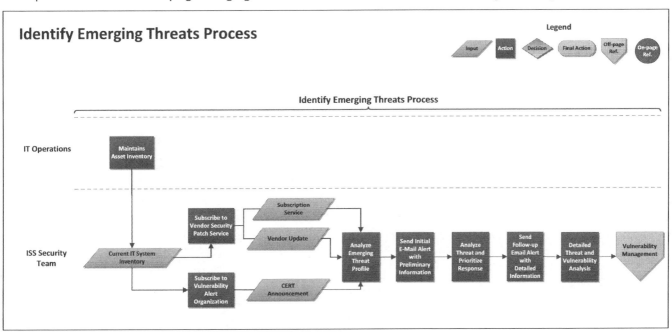

Figure 5. Identify Emerging Threats Process Flow

Identify Emerging Threats Process Steps

Steps in the process for identifying emerging threats are listed in Table 3 below.

Table 3. Identify Emerging Threats Processes

Action	Responsibility
1. **Maintain IT Asset Inventory** – Provide accurate inventory of all IT Assets. Update inventory whenever hardware and/or software is added or removed to ensure inventory is accurate.	IT Operations
2. **Subscribe to Vendor Security Patch Service** – Subscribe to security patch service to ensure security patches for the most current threats are readily available.	IS Security Team
3. **Subscribe to Vulnerability Alerts** – Identify and subscribe to vulnerability notification services that monitor sources of security vulnerability announcements regarding patchable and non-patchable vulnerability remediation for components identified in the IT Asset Inventory.	IS Security Team
4. **Analyze Emerging Threat Profiles** – Continuously evaluate emerging threats and how those threats may impact COMPANY (described in detail below).	IS Security Team
5. **Initial E-Mail Alert** – Send initial e-mail alert to alert distribution list with preliminary information regarding the emerging threat(s).	IS Security Team

Action	**Responsibility**
6. **Analyze Threat and Prioritize Response** – Prioritize appropriate response based on the evaluation in process #4.	IS Security Team
7. **Follow-up E-Mail Alert** – Send follow-up e-mail alert to alert distribution list with detailed information regarding the emerging threat(s).	IS Security Team
8. **Detailed Threat and Vulnerability Analysis** – Prepare detailed analysis of the emerging threat(s) for input to the vulnerability management process.	IS Security Team
9. **Vulnerability Management** – Initiate vulnerability management process.	IS Security Team

Analyze Emerging Threat Profiles

The word "threat" is defined in many different ways by many different organizations. There are several components that make up an overall threat profile. The diagram provided in Figure 6 below shows the relationship between many of the components that make up the emerging threat profile. The lighter stream is an example of profiling a potential zero-day attack. After notification of potential zero-day attacks, it is very important to design and implement security controls to mitigate immediate risk.

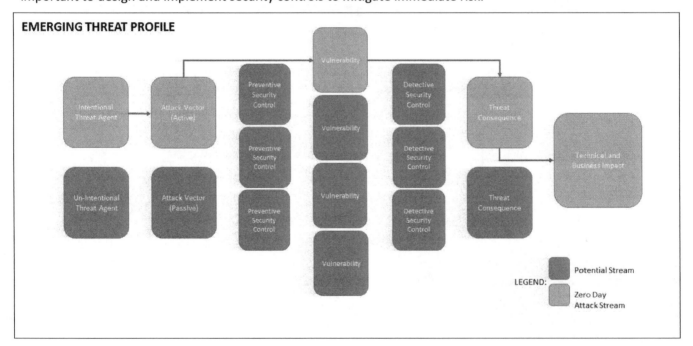

Figure 6. Emerging Threat Profile

The emerging threats landscape is constantly evolving and threat agents are constantly refining their techniques and capabilities. The Threat Management component of the TVM Program provides guidance for monitoring threats and mitigating the risk these threats pose to COMPANY networks. Federal Information Processing Standards Publication 200 (FIPS PUB 200) defines risk as "The level of impact on organizational operations

(including mission, functions, image, or reputation), organizational assets, or individuals resulting from the operation of an information system given the potential impact of a threat and the likelihood of that threat occurring."

According to the SANS Institute, threat management and vulnerability management controls are critical because "Cyber defenders must operate in a constant stream of new information: software updates, patches, security advisories, threat bulletins, etc. Understanding and managing vulnerabilities has become a continuous activity, requiring significant time, attention, and resources. Organizations that do not scan for vulnerabilities and proactively address discovered flaws face a significant likelihood of having their computer systems compromised."

Security Control: Identify Emerging Threats

The importance of identifying emerging threats cannot be overstated. The following control description lists the activities of those responsible for this control. This control maps to the elements of threat management listed in the Threat Management Section of Figure 1. This control is one of the controls expected in a mature TVM Program according to NIST and the SANS Institute.

TVM-IS-C01	**Threat and Vulnerability Management Program**
SOP#: IS TBD	**Title:** Identify Emerging Threats
Date: February 19, 2017	**Basis:** Daily Activity

Control: Subscribe to vulnerability alerting services in order to maintain awareness of emerging threats. Use the information gained from the subscription(s) to update the organization's vulnerability scanning activities on an as needed basis. Also ensure the vulnerability scanning tools being used are updated with new security vulnerability information on a regular basis.

Purpose: Obtaining timely notification of zero-day exploits, new and existing vulnerabilities, and associated remediation solutions is essential for the TVM Program to be effective.

Scope: COMPANY networks.

Frequency: Continuous.

Background: Vendors are the best source for providing intelligence on emerging threats and newly identified vulnerabilities. There are several organizations that provide current information and immediate updates ranging from detecting zero-day-exploits and other newly identified vulnerabilities to providing remediation solutions. Typically, these organizations send alerts as soon as new exploits are detected or when solutions to critical vulnerabilities are made available.

Sources may include:

- Department of Homeland Security Computer Emergency Readiness Team (US-CERT)

- www.us-cert.gov

- National Vulnerability Database web site

- https://nvd.nist.gov/

- National Healthcare and Public Health Information Sharing and Analysis Centers (NH-ISAC)
- Symantec Internet Security Threat Report (ISTR)
- Open Web Application Security Project (OWASP) and other Industry associations
- Software and anti-Virus vendor subscriptions
- Industrial Control Systems Cyber Emergency Response Team (ICS-CERT)
- Forum of Incident Response and Security Teams (FIRST)

Most vendors provide software update support that includes security-patch distribution while others provide security-patch support as an option. Software update and security patch distribution service must be acquired from the vendor, when offered as an option, to ensure product integrity and security. Software and security patches may be distributed via email or as a download from the vendor's support site, to simplify the process of obtaining patches.

Responsibilities:

The IT Operations Team is responsible for tracking IT assets through their acquisition, distribution, use and disposal and for ensuring that all IT Assets conform to applicable COMPANY standards. Effective identification of systems, hardware, and/or software that may be affected by an emerging threat relies upon effective ITAM.

The IS Security Team is responsible for monitoring new threats and vulnerabilities on a continual basis and will ensure COMPANY is subscribed to as many sources of threat and vulnerability information that are deemed appropriate and applicable. Some of the available sources have been referenced above. Processes must be designed and implemented to provide the capability to receive reliable information to facilitate rapid threat identification. The processes must be sufficiently resourced to analyze and act on published threat and vulnerability information. The processes supporting the Identify Emerging Threats control are listed in Table 3 above.

Maturity Levels of Threat Management Activities

As threat management activities become more mature, the level to which they are performed will evolve. Figure 7 below shows the activities that are performed in different Threat Management programs of varying maturity levels.

MIL 1	MIL 2	MIL 3
• Subscribe to threat and vulnerability intelligence services to keep aware of emerging threats, and use the information gained to update the organization's vulnerability scanning activities on a regular basis. • Cybersecurity threat information is gathered and interpreted for the IT function • Threats that are considered important to the function are addressed (e.g., implement mitigating controls, monitor threat status)	• Establish a process to perform threat profiling and risk-rating of threats based on the exploitability and potential impact of the profile. • Threat information sources that address all components of the threat profile are prioritized and monitored • Identified threats are analyzed and prioritized • Threats are addressed according to the assigned priority • The threat profile for the function is validated at an organization-defined frequency	• Correlate event logs and scanning activity. Proactive threat monitoring utilizing a SIEM device that correlates potential threats automatically • Configuration Management tools, such as a FIM, are used to proactively monitor when key configurations have changed potentially threatening the security of the asset • Data Loss Prevention tools are utilized to consistently assess systems that may contain restricted data or when there may have been a data leakage event • Threats profiles are added to a risk register (a structured repository of identified risks) to support risk management activities at an organization-defined frequency
• Subscribe to threat and vulnerability intelligence services to keep aware of emerging threats, and use the information gained to update the organization's vulnerability scanning activities on a regular basis. • Cybersecurity threat information is gathered and interpreted for the IT function • Threats that are considered important to the function are addressed (e.g., implement mitigating controls, monitor threat status)	• Establish a process to perform threat profiling and risk-rating of threats based on the exploitability and potential impact of the profile. • Threat information sources that address all components of the threat profile are prioritized and monitored • Identified threats are analyzed and prioritized • Threats are addressed according to the assigned priority • The threat profile for the function is validated at an organization-defined frequency	• Correlate event logs and scanning activity. Proactive threat monitoring utilizing a SIEM device that correlates potential threats automatically • Configuration Management tools, such as a FIM, are used to proactively monitor when key configurations have changed potentially threatening the security of the asset • Data Loss Prevention tools are utilized to consistently assess systems that may contain restricted data or when there may have been a data leakage event • Threats profiles are added to a risk register (a structured repository of identified risks) to support risk management activities at an organization-defined frequency
MIL 1	MIL 2	MIL 3

Figure 7. Maturity Levels of Threat Management Activities

Vulnerability Management

Vulnerability management is a critical process, or collection of processes, for identifying vulnerabilities to an information system and subsequently removing the vulnerability (also referred to as remediation), or lessening the impact of the vulnerability, or the potential for the vulnerability to be exploited (also referred to as mitigation).

This section will cover the following three aspects of vulnerability management:

- The identification of vulnerabilities utilizing assessment techniques such as vulnerability scanning and penetration testing
- The prioritization of vulnerabilities according to impact level (i.e. critical, high, medium, or low) through the use of a scoring methodology such as the National Vulnerability Database (NVD) Common Vulnerability Scoring System (CVSS)
- The remediation, or mitigation, of vulnerabilities through a structured patch management process; use of hardening techniques to reduce the attack surface of network components, servers, and endpoints; and testing to assess the effectiveness of remediation and/or mitigation techniques.

During his presentation at a large network security conference, the President of the SANS Institute offered the following five axioms regarding vulnerability management:

- Vulnerabilities are the gateways through which threats are manifested.
- Vulnerability scans without remediation have little value.
- A little scanning and remediation is better than a lot of scanning and less remediation.
- Vulnerabilities in need of fixing must be prioritized based on which ones post the most immediate risk to the network.
- Security practitioners need a process that will allow them to stay on the trail of vulnerabilities so the fixes can be more frequent and effective.

Vulnerability Identification

Identifying vulnerabilities is a complex process. An organization's process becomes more mature as the process evolves over time and becomes more well-defined. When vulnerability identification processes are less mature, organizations struggle with things like: knowing the systems and devices to be scanned, establishing the priority of the systems and devices to be scanned, determining how often the systems and devices should be scanned, determining vulnerability remediation priority once the systems and devices have been scanned, and, lastly, refining the overall process to improve operational effectiveness.

Vendor Updates and Subscription Services

In the Threat Management section, vendor updates and subscription services were discussed as one means of identifying emerging threats, zero-day attacks, and new vulnerabilities. Vulnerability alerts, whether from the vendor or a third party, are distributed as new vulnerabilities are discovered. These alerts must be thoroughly analyzed to determine if, and how, the alerts are applicable to the organization's IT assets. Typically, newly discovered vulnerabilities and temporary mitigation instructions are provided through third party subscriber

alerts before vendors provide a solution, usually in the form of a patch. Some alerts are critical and require immediate action.

For example, the "Heartbleed" vulnerability was critical due to pervasive use of the affected software, OpenSSL, combined with potentially significant ramifications for web and email servers if the vulnerability was exploited. The US-CERT website recommended immediate steps to mitigate the vulnerability; however, vendors required more time to isolate, correct, test, and distribute their final remediation solution.

For OS vendors, alerts are typically sent in the form of a patch which may be installed automatically or scheduled for installation at a later time.

Port Scanning

A port scanner, or network mapper, identifies all hosts connected to a network, the network services operating on those hosts, and the specific applications running the identified network services. The port scan provides a comprehensive list of all active hosts, services, printers, switches, and routers operating in the network address space (i.e., any device that contains a network address or is accessible by any other device). The port scanner approved for use on COMPANY networks is Nmap, or Network Mapper.

Nmap is a free, open source tool used to discover, monitor, and troubleshoot TCP/IP-based systems. Nmap is the de facto standard port scanner used by COMPANY technical staff. Nmap is acceptable for host scanning operations on both internal and external (Internet facing) systems supporting COMPANY.

Vulnerability Scanning

Vulnerability scanners are used to scan computer systems, network devices, and applications for vulnerabilities. Typically, scanners identify and assign a score to vulnerabilities using an identification and scoring system such as the NVD CVSS. The majority of known vulnerabilities are listed in the NVD and CVSS scores are used to assign a severity level to the vulnerabilities. This allows an organization to prioritize remediation activities according to the severity of the vulnerability.

Severity levels based on CVSS scores are listed below:

- Vulnerabilities are labeled "Critical" severity for CVSS base score of 10
- Vulnerabilities are labeled "High" severity for CVSS base score of 7.0 – 9.9
- Vulnerabilities are labeled "Medium" severity for CVSS base score of 4.0 – 6.9
- Vulnerabilities are labeled "Low" severity for CVSS base score of 0.0 – 3.9

Most vulnerability scanners provide solutions for remediating vulnerabilities discovered during the scan. The solution may be a security patch or it may be a configuration change such as disabling certain services.

The vulnerability scanners approved for use on COMPANY networks are listed below.

- The Nessus Vulnerability Scanner, from Tenable Corporation, has been approved for internal vulnerability scans of COMPANY networks. Standard Operating Procedure (SOP) #IS0007 (Network Scanning) provides instructions on how to use Nessus.

- Retina CS, from BeyondTrust, has been approved for external (i.e., Internet facing) vulnerability scans of COMPANY networks. SOP #IS0007 (Network Scanning) provides instructions on how to use Retina CS.

Security Control: Identify Vulnerabilities – Network Scanning

Network vulnerability scanning is a key security control that involves an automated process of proactively identifying security vulnerabilities of systems and devices connected to enterprise networks to determine if and how the systems can be exploited.

Network scanning employs highly specialized software tools to identify vulnerabilities based on a database of known vulnerabilities such as the NVD, to test systems and devices for the existence of these vulnerabilities, and to generate a report of the findings. Vulnerability analysts and other technical staff members use the report to remediate or mitigate the vulnerabilities and thereby enhance the overall security of the network.

TVM-IS-C02	**Threat and Vulnerability Management Program**
SOP#: IS0007	**Title:** Identify Vulnerabilities – Network Scanning
Date: February 19, 2017	**Basis:** Organizational Defined Activity

Control: Run vulnerability scanning tools against all systems and devices on internal and external networks on a pre-defined schedule. Deliver prioritized lists of identified vulnerabilities to IT Operations along with risk scores to facilitate remediation and mitigation activities to reduce overall risk to COMPANY networks. Use a Security Content Automation Protocol (SCAP)-validated vulnerability scanner that detects both code-based vulnerabilities, such as those described in the Common Vulnerabilities and Exposures (CVE) database, and configuration-based vulnerabilities, such as those enumerated in the Common Configuration Enumeration (CCE) database.

Purpose: Identify vulnerabilities on COMPANY networks.

Scope: COMPANY networks.

Frequency: Quarterly.

Background: The following tools and software are needed for port and vulnerability scanning:

Port and network scanning tools: Nmap, Nessus, and Retina CS

Additional software required: Cygwin, including SQLite, Python, R, GCC-g++, make. In R, install.packages("RSQLite"), TTF Fonts and Notepad++

Responsibilities:

The Office of Compliance Services (OCS) will maintain the SOP for performing vulnerability scanning.

The Compliance Manager is responsible for ensuring scans are run on a pre-defined schedule to establish a listing of vulnerabilities. The list of vulnerabilities will be input into Service Now, a cloud-based service

management tool, to create a ticket to establish the timestamp for when the listing was created. The Service Now ticket is then passed to the IS Security Team.

The IT Operations Team is responsible for internal vulnerability scanning. They will conduct scanning and remediation activities according to the directives of the TVM Program.

The IS Security Team is responsible for vulnerability analysis, prioritization, and remediation as well as coordinating patch management activities in support of vulnerability remediation. The Team is also responsible for ensuring objectives in Service Level Agreements (SLAs) for vulnerability remediation are being achieved and for notifying the HSSC when the potential for not achieving SLA objectives is imminent. The Team is also responsible for closing out Service Now tickets and for communicating with OCS when remediation activities are concluded to allow OCS to initiate rescans to verify vulnerabilities have been remediated.

Security Control: Identify Vulnerabilities – Network Penetration Testing

Penetration testing or "pen testing" is a simulated attack on network systems and devices using known attack vectors. The objective of pen testing is to verify vulnerabilities identified through network scanning are exploitable along with finding new vulnerabilities not identified through network scanning.

Authorized individuals performing pen testing attempt to circumvent the security features of network security appliances, systems, and devices through the use of tools and techniques typically used by malicious attackers based on the pen tester's understanding of the network design and implementation of security features on the network security appliances, systems, and devices connected to the network.

The goal of pen testing is to identify and remediate, or mitigate, vulnerabilities before malicious attackers find and exploit the vulnerabilities. This approach will enhance the overall security posture of COMPANY networks. The HIPAA Security Rule does not specifically require pen testing for compliance. However, pen testing should be used in conjunction with vulnerability scanning because vulnerability scanners are known to miss a number of critical vulnerabilities that would be discovered through pen testing.

The following types of penetration testing can be performed to discover vulnerabilities:

- Wired Network Penetration Testing
- Wireless Network Penetration Testing
- Web Application Penetration Testing
- VoIP/Telephony Penetration Testing
- Social Engineering Penetration Testing
- Physical Penetration Testing

TVM-IS-C03	**Threat and Vulnerability Management Program**
SOP#: IS TBD	**Title:** Identify Vulnerabilities – Network Penetration Testing
Date: February 19, 2017	**Basis:** Organizational Defined Activity

Control: At a minimum, pen testing will be performed on an annual basis to identify exploitable vulnerabilities and as required to verify vulnerabilities previously identified and remediated have, in fact, been remediated. Verification is accomplished by comparing results of pen testing with vulnerability scan reports and/or prior pen testing results.

Purpose: Employ individuals with highly specialized skill sets that use highly specialized tools to simulate malicious attackers to identify exploitable vulnerabilities before a malicious attacker finds and exploits the vulnerability possibly resulting in the unauthorized disclosure, modification, or destruction of Restricted Information.

Scope: COMPANY networks.

Frequency: Annually and as necessary to confirm vulnerability remediation.

Background: Currently, proposals have been solicited to outsource pen testing of COMPANY networks to a vendor with the requisite skills and experience.

Responsibilities:

The Office of Compliance Services (OCS) will maintain the SOP for performing pen testing.

The Compliance Manager is responsible for ensuring pen tests are performed at least annually to identify vulnerabilities or as needed to verify vulnerability remediation. The list of vulnerabilities identified from pen testing will be input into Service Now to create a ticket to establish the timestamp for the listing. The list is then provided to the IS Security Team.

The IS Security Team is responsible for ensuring vulnerabilities identified during pen testing are remediated in accordance with COMPANY policy. The Team is also responsible for ensuring objectives in SLAs for penetration testing are being achieved and for notifying the HSSC when the potential for not achieving SLA objectives is imminent. The Team is also responsible for closing out Service Now tickets and for communicating with OCS when remediation activities are concluded to allow OCS to initiate pen testing as may be necessary from time to time to verify vulnerability remediation

The Vendor selected to perform pen testing is responsible for performing pen testing and providing results to the IS Security Team.

Vulnerability Prioritization

Each vulnerability and the potential impact to COMPANY networks if the vulnerability is discovered and exploited by a malicious attacker must be considered when scoring vulnerabilities to establish remediation priority. Prioritizing vulnerabilities involves determining the overall threat profile as discussed in the Threat Management section, grouping known vulnerabilities by severity category, understanding where Restricted Information may exist, and understanding which systems are considered essential systems.

As previously mentioned, CVSS scores are used to determine the severity of vulnerabilities. Vulnerabilities rated as "Critical" or "High" severity are given first priority for remediation.

- Vulnerabilities are labeled "Critical" severity for CVSS base score of 10.0

- Vulnerabilities are labeled "High" severity for CVSS base score of 7.0 – 9.9
- Vulnerabilities are labeled "Medium" severity for CVSS base score of 4.0 – 6.9
- Vulnerabilities are labeled "Low" severity for CVSS base score of 0.0 – 3.9

Next, the risk or exposure of the systems themselves must be considered. As a healthcare organization, most COMPANY systems are classified "essential" or "necessary" and most will process or store ePHI. Accordingly, those systems are subject to compliance with the HIPAA Security Rule.

The order of priority for remediation of vulnerabilities identified on COMPANY networks is listed below:

- Externally facing systems most vulnerable to attack from outside of the network;
- Systems interfacing with CareConnect;
- CareConnect itself; and
- Everything else.

The vulnerability remediation priority strategy for CY 2017, as agreed upon by COMPANY stakeholders, is depicted in Figure 9 below.

Figure 9. Vulnerability Remediation Priority Strategy for CY 2017

After identifying and prioritizing vulnerabilities, the next step is analyzing the vulnerabilities to gain a better understanding of the overall risk to COMPANY networks, determining which vulnerabilities can be remediated, and determining what is involved in remediation. For vulnerabilities that cannot be remediated, compensating controls (e.g., isolating the affected system on a separate network) may exist and must be considered. Lastly, the level of acceptable risk must be determined along with the process for obtaining approval to accept risk in cases where vulnerabilities cannot be remediated or mitigated and for which there are no compensating controls.

Security Control: Confirm Vulnerability Prioritization

TVM-IS-C04	**Threat and Vulnerability Management Program**
SOP#: IS TBD	**Title:** Confirm Vulnerability Prioritization
Date: February 19, 2017	**Basis:** Organizational Defined Activity

Control: Establish a process to determine vulnerability remediation priority based on severity levels derived from CVSS scores along with the strategy for vulnerability remediation priority for 2017 agreed upon by COMPANY stakeholders. The prioritized vulnerability remediation list should be grouped by asset category (e.g., servers in the DMZ, internal network servers, switches, routers, desktops, laptops, etc.).

Purpose: Determine the priority for remediating vulnerabilities identified through network scanning and pen testing.

Scope: COMPANY networks.

Frequency: After vulnerability scans and pen tests.

Background: Some software applications will be tied to specific OS versions. If the OS cannot be upgraded because the vendor does not support a newer version of the OS, the IS Security Team must determine what, if any, compensating controls can be deployed (e.g., isolating these systems on a separate network). If compensating controls cannot be deployed, a determination must be made as to whether or not the risk of leaving the vulnerable system connected to the network is acceptable. Acceptance of risk must be approved by OCS.

Responsibilities:

The Office of Compliance Services (OCS) approves acceptable risk when a determination is made that systems with vulnerabilities that cannot be remediated or mitigated with compensating controls must remain connected to the network.

The Compliance Manager approves the vulnerability remediation priority list.

The IS Security Team is responsible for verifying calculated risk scores from vulnerability scan results by assessing the affected systems' exposure and criticality to COMPANY networks and combining that data with CVSS scores listed in vulnerability scanning reports. Once prioritized by risk score, the Team will coordinate with the Compliance Manager to approve the remediation priority list and will coordinate with IT Operations to remediate vulnerabilities according to the priority list.

Vulnerability Remediation

The timeframe between identifying, analyzing, and prioritizing vulnerabilities and the amount of time it takes for remediating, or mitigating, those vulnerabilities must be kept as short as possible. The longer it takes to remediate a known vulnerability, the larger the window of opportunity for a potential attacker to exploit the vulnerability.

Vulnerability remediation typically involves a combination of applying security patches and employing hardening techniques to configure systems in the most secure manner possible. For example, typical OS installations on application servers yields many processes that run when the server is booted. Some of the processes are not necessary (i.e. they are "redundant") for the correct operation of the application installed on the server. Redundant processes are considered to be vulnerabilities because they are potential vectors for a malicious attack.

A process is currently being documented for dealing with vulnerabilities that cannot be remediated by applying a security patch or through server hardening techniques (i.e., disabling redundant processes). In some cases, compensating controls may be necessary to mitigate vulnerabilities that cannot otherwise be remediated or mitigated in some systems. In those cases, it is imperative to isolate these systems on a separate network.

As previously stated, vulnerability scanning and pen testing are used to identify vulnerabilities on COMPANY networks. After vulnerabilities have been remediated by applying security patches or through the use of server hardening techniques, systems are re-scanned, or pen testing on the system is performed, to verify

vulnerabilities identified in the previous scan or pen test have, in fact, been remediated (.i.e., patching or hardening was successful.)

The security patching process, not to be confused with scheduled system updates, may be automatic or manual. Efforts are underway to automate manual patching procedures. Currently, only vulnerabilities assigned Critical or High severity are being remediated while the remaining vulnerabilities assigned Medium or Low severity are entered into a Plan of Action and Milestones (POA&M) and scheduled for remediation at a later date.

Patch Management

Patch management is a process for identifying, acquiring, installing, and verifying patches and/or hot fixes for systems on COMPANY networks. Patches correct security vulnerabilities, fix functionality problems, or add new functionality in both OS and application software. In some cases, patches fix firmware issues. Of the various types of patches, security patches, in particular, are of very high interest in the TVM Program. Applying security patches remediates vulnerabilities thereby significantly reducing the risk those vulnerabilities will be exploited which enhances the overall security posture of COMPANY networks.

In accordance with policy HS 9457, Minimum Security Standards for Network Devices, Appendix I – Device Configuration Standard, patches and hot fixes must be installed as soon as possible but no later than three months after release. Patches/hot fixes deemed critical must be applied within seven business days. Systems that cannot be patched must be on isolated subnets.

Appendix II of the policy covers publicly accessible devices. For devices in the DMZ, all critical patches and hot fixes must be installed as soon as possible but no later than one month after their release or within 24 hours of notification by Medical Information Technology Services (MITS) or School of Medicine Information Technology Services (SOMITS).

The IT Operations Team is responsible for downloading patches, including security patches, to be applied to systems in both the Lab and Production Environment.

If a large number of patches need to be applied, a phased rollout can be employed to minimize impact to affected networks. Patches for vulnerabilities rated Critical should be applied first followed by patches for vulnerabilities rated High.

A SOP for applying emergency security patches directly to production systems should be developed.

Lastly, it should be noted the patch management function is not included in the TVM Program. Additional details about patch management can be found in applicable documents and/or runbooks.

Patch management for specific OS versions is described below:

- Windows 7 – Desktop OS patches are deployed by the Lumension endpoint management tool and is administered by the local desktop manager. Desktops are configured to receive updates from the local desktop manager rather than Microsoft's automated update services.
- Windows Server – Server OS patches are deployed by Microsoft's Windows Server Update Services (WSUS) managed by Windows Server Manager.

- SUSE Linux – Patches are applied manually by the *nix Manager once per month or when deemed appropriate.
- Red Hat Linux – Patches are applied manually by the *nix Manager once per month or when deemed appropriate.
- IBM AIX – Patches are applied manually by the*nix Manager once per month or when deemed appropriate.
- Apple – Patches for all Apple equipment running any version of any Apple OS must be kept up to date. Apple equipment includes, but is not limited to, the following: MacBooks, iMacs, Mac Minis, iPads, and iPhones. Detailed procedures for device administration and patching are under development at this time.

Regarding new OS releases and patches, BFB–IS–3, Electronic Information Security Policy, states that "Patch management in conformance with change management processes... and campus minimum standards... Systems personnel should, in a timely manner, update versions of the operating system and application software for which security patches are made available."

Security Control: Confirm Vulnerability Remediation

TVM-IS-C05	Threat and Vulnerability Management Program
SOP#: IS TBD	Title: Confirm Vulnerability Remediation
Date: February 19, 2017	Basis: Organizational Defined Activity

Control: Compare the results from back-to-back vulnerability scans or pen tests to verify that vulnerabilities were remediated either by patching, implementing a compensating control (e.g., isolating the vulnerable system), or documenting and accepting a reasonable business risk. Such acceptance of business risks for existing vulnerabilities should be periodically reviewed to determine if newer compensating controls or subsequent patches can address vulnerabilities that were previously accepted, or if conditions have changed, increasing the risk.

Purpose: Confirm remediation of vulnerabilities on COMPANY networks identified through vulnerability scans and/or pen tests. Confirmation is typically obtained by rescanning systems that contained vulnerabilities identified through a prior scan or by performing another pen test on those systems.

Scope: COMPANY networks.

Frequency: Upon completion of remediation activities.

Background: As previous stated, many vulnerabilities are remediated through the application of security patches which is often an automated process. It is not prudent to assume automated security patch application tools successfully remediated all vulnerabilities expected, or intended, to be remediated by the security patches. Therefore, to minimize the risk all vulnerabilities were not successfully remediated, the most prudent course of action is to perform a rescan and/or conduct another pen test to confirm the expected, or intended, vulnerabilities were, in fact, successfully remediated.

Responsibilities:

The Compliance Manager will coordinate analysis of reports from scanning and pen testing to confirm vulnerability remediation has taken place in satisfaction of applicable policies.

The IT Operations Team will be responsible for ensuring rescans of internal systems occur in a timely manner.

The IS Security Team will be responsible for ensuring rescans and/or pen tests of external systems occur in a timely manner and that vulnerability analysts confirm vulnerability remediation on both external and internal systems was successful.

Vulnerability Isolation

Occasionally, vulnerabilities may be discovered that cannot be remediated by applying security patches or through hardening techniques. In those cases, it may be possible to mitigate the vulnerabilities through the implementation of compensating controls.

If compensating controls cannot be found, it will be necessary to protect the network from itself by isolating systems that contain vulnerabilities on untrusted networks.

The philosophy behind isolating vulnerable systems is to treat sections of the network where vulnerable systems are connected as "untrusted networks." Any traffic passing between the "untrusted" networks and the "trusted" (i.e. secure) network must be tightly controlled to prevent anyone or anything from exploiting the vulnerabilities that exist on the systems on the untrusted network. It is important to note that isolation of vulnerable systems is not a perfect solution; but, it is better than the alternative of leaving vulnerable systems on the trusted network and running the risk of a malicious attacker finding and exploiting the vulnerable systems. All data should be encrypted as it leaves the untrusted network and should be scanned for errors and/or malicious attacks as it enters the trusted network.

In the current threat landscape where malicious attackers are working literally around the clock to break into networks to steal anything they can, it is of utmost importance to be prepared to isolate vulnerable systems on untrusted networks to prevent the unauthorized disclosure, modification, or destruction of Restricted Information.

In accordance with Policy IV of HS 9457, "Devices that cannot be protected in the required manner (virus scanning, spyware/adware protection, patch updates, secure configuration) must be located in protected subnets or isolated by other approved means. Such systems would include, but would not be limited to, turn-key systems on which the vendor prohibits any 3rd party software and operating system patches and legacy systems that cannot be updated."

High-Level Vulnerability Management Process Flow

At a very high level, vulnerability management is simply about identifying, prioritizing, remediating, and, if necessary, isolating vulnerabilities and then repeating that process on a continuous basis to drive down the number of vulnerabilities beginning with those rated Critical or High (See Figure 10). There will be instances of vulnerabilities that cannot be remediated or mitigated, for one reason or another. In those cases, it may be necessary to isolate the vulnerable systems on untrusted networks. Access to the untrusted networks to which

the vulnerable systems are connected must be tightly controlled (i.e., restricted to only those who must access the systems in the course of performing their daily duties).

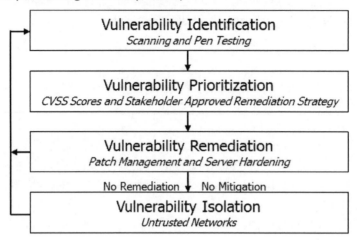

Figure 10. High-Level Vulnerability Management Process Flow

Vulnerability Management Process Flow Diagram

The process flow for vulnerability management is illustrated in the Swim Lane Diagram in Figure 11 below.

Threat and Vulnerability Management Program

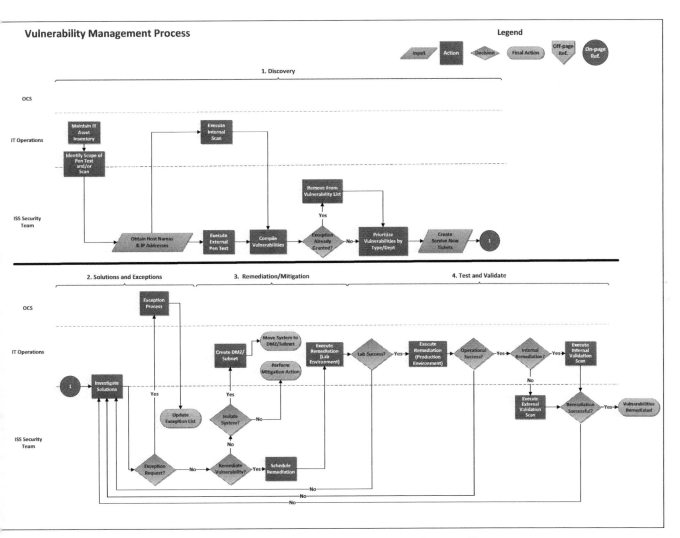

Figure 11. Vulnerability Management Process Flow

Vulnerability Management Process Steps

Steps in the vulnerability management process flow are listed in Table 4 below.

Table 4. Vulnerability Management Process

Action	Responsibility
Maintain IT Asset Inventory — Provide accurate inventory of all IT Assets. Update inventory based on adding or removing hardware and/or software to ensure inventory is accurate.	IT Operations

	Date:	Owner:
	Version #: 1.0	Page #: 34 of 52

Threat and Vulnerability Management Program

Action	Responsibility
Identify Scope of Internal Scan and/or External Pen Test — IT Operations and the IS Security Team will collaborate to identify the host names and/or IP address ranges for internal scans and/or external scans/pen tests.	IT Operations IS Security Team
Obtain Host Names/IP Addresses — Prepare list of internal and external host names and IP addresses for internal scans and/or external scans/pen tests.	IS Security Team
Execute Internal Scan — IT Operations will execute internal scans. Go to step 6.	IT Operations
Execute External Pen Test — The IS Security Team will oversee the execution of external scans/pen tests by a service provider.	IS Security Team
Compile Vulnerabilities — Findings from internal scans and external scans/pen tests will be aggregated in a database or other tracking tool to facilitate centralized management of vulnerabilities.	IS Security Team
Exception Already Granted? — The IS Security Team will check the Exception List to determine if an exception has already been granted for vulnerabilities identified during internal scans and/or external scans/pen tests. If an exception has not already been granted, go to step 9.	IS Security Team
Remove From Vulnerability List — Vulnerabilities will be removed from the list for which an exception has already been granted.	IS Security Team
Prioritize Vulnerabilities by Type/Dept. — A risk-rating algorithm (i.e., asset exposure/risk, CVSS score, threat landscape, etc.) will be used to prioritize vulnerabilities by type and department that would have the most severe impact on COMPANY networks.	IS Security Team
Create Service Now Tickets — The IS Security Team will create Service Now tickets to date and time stamp the compiled list of vulnerabilities. A master ticket will be created along with separate, subordinate tickets for each department.	IS Security Team
Investigate Solutions — IT Operations and the IS Security Team will collaborate on appropriate solutions to identified vulnerabilities and obtain stakeholder buy-in.	IT Operations IS Security Team
Exception Request — If a solution is not readily available (e.g., security patch is not available), the IS Security Team will forward an exception request to OCS. If an exception request is not necessary, go to step 15.	IS Security Team
Exception Process — OCS will review the exception request and either approve the exception or deny the exception.	OCS
Update Exception List — The IS Security Team will update the Exception List for vulnerabilities for which exceptions have been approved.	IS Security Team
Remediate Vulnerability? — For vulnerabilities that cannot be remediated, mitigation actions may be necessary. If the vulnerability can be remediated, go to step 20.	IS Security Team

34   <Company>   CONFIDENTIAL   <Website>

Threat and Vulnerability Management Program

Action	Responsibility
Isolate System? — For vulnerabilities that cannot be remediated or mitigated, it will be necessary to isolate the vulnerable systems from the main network. If mitigation action is possible, go to step 19.	IS Security Team
Create DMZ/Subnet — A DMZ/Subnet will be created for the vulnerable system(s).	IT Operations
Move System to DMZ/Subnet — The vulnerable system(s) are moved to the DMZ/Subnet.	IT Operations
Perform Mitigation Action — IT Operations will perform mitigation actions (configuration changes, additional security controls, increased monitoring, etc.) as applicable.	IT Operations
Schedule Remediation — The IS Security Team will coordinate with affected departments to schedule remediation.	IS Security Team
Execute Remediation (Lab Environment) — Remediation actions are performed and tested in the Lab Environment.	IT Operations
Lab Success? — If remediation actions were successful in the Lab Environment, remediation can now be done in the Production Environment. Otherwise, go to step 11.	IT Operations
Execute Remediation (Production Environment) —Perform remediation actions in the Production Environment.	IT Operations
Operational Success? — If the host/application could be successfully rebooted/restarted, the remediation action must be validated. If the host/application could not be successfully rebooted/restarted, go to step 11.	IT Operations
Internal Remediation? — Was remediation performed on an internal or external system? If remediation was performed on an external system, go to step 26.	IT Operations
Execute Internal Validation Scan — Execute an internal scan to validate vulnerabilities were remediated. Go to step 27.	IT Operations
Execute External Validation Scan — Execute an external scan to validate vulnerabilities were remediated.	IS Security Team
Remediation Successful? — If vulnerabilities were not successfully remediated, go to step 11.	IS Security Team
Vulnerabilities Remediated	IS Security Team

Demilitarized Zone (DMZ) Implementation

At this time, a DMZ does not exist. Creation of a DMZ is underway. Once the DMZ has been created, external facing hosts can be added to the DMZ.

A dual-homed gateway architecture is recommended. This is more commonly known as a dual firewall DMZ implementation. This requires putting an external firewall between the Internet and the DMZ and another firewall between the DMZ and the internal LAN.

It is further recommended the firewalls be from different vendors. The rationale is that malicious traffic not detected by one of the firewalls may be detected by the other.

Another aspect that bears consideration is to create separate zones for internal database servers that must be accessed from the DMZ. This would require traffic between the DMZ and database serves to pass through yet another firewall. If any of the database servers are compromised, the rest of the internal network cannot be accessed from the zone that contains any compromised database servers.

Vulnerability Management Cycle Timeline

The vulnerability management process is a cycle that repeats on a quarterly basis as depicted in Figure 12 below.

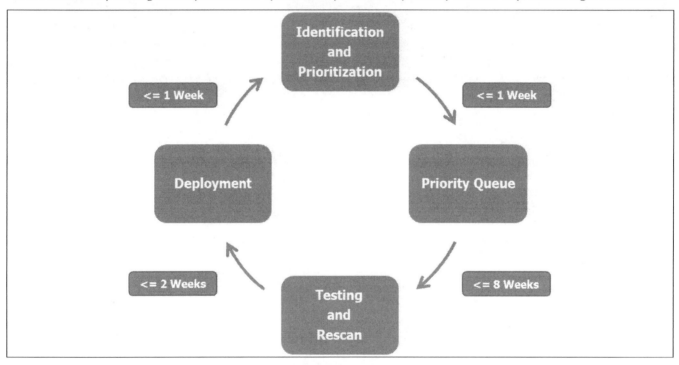

Figure 12. Vulnerability Management Process Timeline

Maturity Levels of Vulnerability Management Activities

As vulnerability management activities and processes mature, the level to which they are performed will evolve. Figure 13 below shows the activities performed in different vulnerability management programs of varying maturities.

- Information sources to support vulnerability discovery have been identified (e.g., US-CERT, various critical infrastructure sector ISACs, ICS-CERT, industry associations, vendors, federal briefings, internal assessments)

- Vulnerability information is gathered and interpreted for various IT functions

- Vulnerabilities that are considered important to the function are addressed

MIL 1

- Vulnerability information sources that address all assets important to IT functions are monitored

- Security vulnerability assessments are performed (e.g., architectural reviews, penetration testing, cybersecurity exercises, vulnerability scanning)

- Identified security vulnerabilities are analyzed and prioritized (e.g., NIST Common Vulnerability Scoring System could be used for patches; internal guidelines could be used to prioritize other types of vulnerabilities)

- Security vulnerabilities are addressed according to the assigned priority

- Operational impact to IT functions are evaluated prior to deploying security patches

MIL 2

- Security vulnerability assessments are performed for all assets on an organization-defined frequency

- Vulnerability assessments are performed by parties that are independent of the TVM function

- Analysis and prioritization of cybersecurity vulnerabilities are informed by the function's (or organization's) risk criteria

- Vulnerability information is added to the risk register

- Risk monitoring activities validate the remediation of security vulnerabilities within an organization-defined frequency or SLA

MIL 3

Figure 13. Maturity Levels of Vulnerability Management Activities

Supporting Security Controls

The threat and vulnerability management security controls described in previous sections are the heart of the TVM Program and essential to its success.

However, the TVM Program is but one of many components of the overall security program established to enhance the security of COMPANY networks.

Accordingly, deployment of additional controls will be necessary to support a comprehensive security program

Fundamental Network Security Architecture Controls

Many IT security professionals consider the controls described below to be fundamental components of the security architecture of any network.

Access Control List (ACLs) and Firewall Rulesets

Access control lists (ACLs) are lists of permissions attached to objects (i.e., devices connected to a network). An ACL specifies which users or system processes are granted access to objects, as well as the operations allowed on those objects.

A firewall is a network security appliance that controls inbound and outbound network traffic based on a set of rules typically referred to as a ruleset. Firewall rulesets define the network traffic allowed to enter or leave the

network and the traffic not allowed to enter or leave the network, typically expressed as traffic that is "permitted or denied."

ACLs and firewall rulesets for processing inbound and outbound network traffic for specific IP addresses and IP address ranges, protocols, applications, and content type based on the organization's information security policies must be reviewed on a periodic basis. Structured change control should be applied for any changes made to ACLs or firewall rulesets.

Encryption

Encryption is the appropriate logical security measure for protecting Restricted Information on servers and/or endpoints from unauthorized access. Encryption must be applied to Restricted Information when stored on any device connected to COMPANY networks and when the Restricted Information moves through the network. The former is typically referred to as Data at Rest and the latter is typically referred to as Data in Motion.

The Advanced Encryption Standard (AES) and Triple Data Encryption Algorithm (TDEA), the common name for which is Triple Data Encryption Standard (3DES), are two of many cryptographic algorithms approved for use by NIST. AES is widely available and, when used, should be used in FIPS-140 mode. If any other cryptographic algorithm is to be used, justification for using the other algorithm must be provided to OCS and a waiver must be approved.

Data at Rest

Data at rest is encrypted Restricted Information stored on desktops, laptops, tablets, databases, file servers, and backup storage media. Additionally, subsets of Restricted Information can often be found in log files, application files, configuration files, and many other places.

Encryption Techniques:

- Full Disk Encryption — Full disk encryption (FDE), also known as whole disk encryption, is the process of encrypting all data on the hard drive used to boot a computer, including the OS, and permitting access to the data only after successful authentication to the FDE application. Pre-boot authentication occurs when the FDE application prompts the user to provide authentication credentials, such as entering a user ID and password, before decrypting all the data on the hard drive and allowing the boot process to complete. This is the preferred method. Other products require the user to authenticate after the OS has booted, which provides weaker protection than pre-boot authentication but is acceptable.
- File, Folder, and Database Encryption — File encryption is the process of encrypting individual files on storage media and permitting access to the encrypted data only after proper authentication credentials are provided. Folder encryption is very similar to file encryption except all files contained within the folder are encrypted. Database encryption is another technique for protecting Restricted Information in databases by encrypting all data files associated with the database application.
- Backup Storage Media Encryption — Restricted Information is a high priority target of hackers, especially the type of data that can be used for financial fraud and medical identity theft. Compliance with the HIPAA Security Rule requires encrypting all backup storage media. Accordingly, all backup storage media containing any Restricted Information.

Data in Motion

Data in motion is Restricted Information moving from one system to another. Both systems may exist within the boundaries of COMPANY networks, or either system may exist in an "untrusted" network such as the Internet. When in motion, Restricted Information must be encrypted using one of the techniques described below. A justification for any exception must be submitted to OCS and a waiver must be approved.

Encryption Techniques:

- SSL/TLS — Both the Secure Sockets Layer (SSL) version 3.0 and Transport Layer Security (TLS) version 1.0 protocol specifications use cryptographic mechanisms to implement security services for establishing and maintaining secure Transport Control Protocol/Internet Protocol (TCP/IP) connections. Secure connections prevent eavesdropping, tampering, or message forgery. Providing confidentiality through the use of encryption prevents eavesdropping; generating a message authentication code with a secure hash function prevents undetected tampering; and, authenticating clients and servers with public key cryptography-based digital signatures prevents message forgery.
- SFTP — Secure Shell (SSH) File Transfer Protocol (SFTP) is a network protocol for securely accessing and managing files on remote file systems. This is not to be confused with running Simple File Transfer Protocol, an unsecure version of File Transfer Protocol (FTP), through a secured channel. It is strongly recommended that usage of FTP be replaced with the latest version of SFTP.
- SSH — Secure Shell (SSH) is a protocol for logging into a remote host and executing commands on that host (e.g., administrative commands). The SSH protocol differs from earlier remote administration protocols, such as telnet, remote shell (rsh), remote login (rlogin), and remote copy (rcp), because SSH provides built-in support for robust security features such as user authentication, device authentication, and transmission encryption. SSH has almost completely taken the place of earlier remote administration protocols. SSH-based automated access management with a strong focus on security is the current direction of the network security industry. It is strongly recommended that any use of telnet, rsh, rlogin, or rcp be replaced with the latest version of SSH.
- HTTPS — Hypertext Transfer Protocol Secure (HTTPS) is a communications protocol for secure communication over computer networks, with particularly wide deployment on the Internet. Web browsers such as Internet Explorer, Mozilla, Firefox, Chrome, and Apple Safari are installed on almost all computers connected to the Internet and all of these browsers support HTTPS. Technically, HTTPS is not a protocol in and of itself; rather, it is the result of simply layering the Hypertext Transfer Protocol (HTTP) on top of the SSL/TLS protocol, thus adding SSL/TLS security features to the standard HTTP implementation. The main motivation for HTTPS is to prevent eavesdropping and man-in-the-middle (MITM) attacks. Configuring the preferred web browser to use AES encryption with a key length of 128-bits is highly recommended and a key length of 256-bits is preferred.

Data Loss Prevention (DLP)

Data Loss Prevention (DLP) tools monitor Restricted Information internally or at network boundaries for unusual or suspicious events or transfers of information. DLP tools are also utilized to discover where Restricted Information exists on COMPANY networks and to identify users who have access to the Restricted Information.

It is important to note that if the location of Restricted Information is not known, it cannot be adequately protected.

DLP, as the name suggests, is a preventive measure organizations can implement to mitigate the risk of unauthorized disclosure, modification, or destruction of Restricted Information. If a DLP-based tool is in place to prevent Restricted Information, such as ePHI, from being copied from an endpoint, e-mailed outside of the network, or leaked via a web application, the threat of such a security breach occurring is lessened considerably. If a DLP-based tool is in place to search for, detect, and report where Restricted Information may exist, the organization is equipped with the means to ensure adequate security measures have been taken and that only appropriate, trusted individuals have access to the data.

Malware Protection

Malware protection consists of two aspects:

- Anti-virus (AV) software products prevent files containing viruses from being downloaded onto a computer. Many AV products also try to prevent the virus from being activated and placed in memory or in a file-like location.
- Malware software products remove viruses and malware from an infected computer, should a virus or other malware somehow pass through an antivirus software check.

File Integrity Monitoring (FIM)

File Integrity Monitoring (FIM) is a control that validates the integrity of OS and application software files using a verification method to compare the current state of files against a known, good baseline. This enables organizations to better protect against malware attacks that could result in the unauthorized disclosure, modification, or destruction of Restricted Information by closely monitoring file access and modification.

The scope of FIM is not limited to only the content contained in system and application files and folders, but also the integrity of registry key/value pairs in Windows operating systems.

FIM solutions proactively identify when changes to key files have occurred which indicates a malicious attack may have occurred. One of the key benefits of a FIM solution is an alert is sent to the management console as soon as the change is detected as opposed to not discovering the vulnerability that allowed the change to be made until a vulnerability scan is performed perhaps weeks or months after the change was made.

It is important to note that FIM is a process parallel to the vulnerability management process. Technically, changes to files detected by FIM should be considered a breach as opposed to a vulnerability. Alerts generated by FIM solutions should be routed to the Computer Security Incident Response Team (CSIRT) for analysis and response.

To ensure the security and integrity of data at rest and data in motion, COMPANY is required to deploy a FIM solution to comply with the HIPAA Security Rule.

The following steps are required to implement FIM:

- Establish a baseline of message digest values (i.e., hash values) for the files, folders, and, for Windows-based systems, registry key/value pairs.
- When changes are detected (.i.e., a monitored file or registry key/value pair is modified), the FIM application generates alerts to indicate the message digest of a monitored file differs from the message digest in the baseline. Malware and Advanced Persistent Threats (APTs) typically access or modify OS and application files. Automated FIM tools will detect the changes and send an alert to the management console that indicates a malicious attacker may have found and exploited an existing vulnerability that has yet to be remediated or has conducted a zero-day attack.
- Re-establish the baseline of message digest values after authorized modifications have been made (e.g., installing a new version of OS or application software, applying security patches to remediate vulnerabilities, etc.).

Intrusion Detection Systems and Intrusion Prevention Systems (IDS/IPS)

Intrusion Detection Systems and Intrusion Prevention Systems (IDS/IPS) should be deployed to monitor COMPANY networks for potentially malicious network traffic. These systems can detect security policy violations and generate alerts to a management console. In some cases, an IDS/IPS may be able to prevent suspected malicious traffic from entering the network, depending on the capabilities of the system. There are both network-based and host-based IDS/IPS and each are designed to accomplish specific objectives.

Secure Web Application Coding and Web Application Firewalls (WAF)

Secure web application development standards, along with static and dynamic code testing, are security controls for ensuring web applications are developed with structured and secure coding practices such as those advocated by organizations like the Open Web Application Security Project (OWASP). Secure coding practices and code reviews are beneficial preventive measures to ensure common and widespread threats such as Cross-Site Scripting (XSS) and SQL injection are identified and resolved before web applications are put in the production environment. Secure coding practices and code reviews are proactive measures used in more mature TVM Programs.

More mature IT organizations also implement Web Application Firewalls (WAFs) that analyze traffic in the application layer (OSI Layer 7) to protect web applications from harmful attacks. WAFs can often detect potentially harmful activities that an IDS/IPS is unable to detect.

Threat/Log Monitoring

The threat and log monitoring function is typically accomplished through the use of Security Information and Event Management (SIEM) tools. These tools centralize the task of aggregating, consolidating, and correlating log files from multiple network devices and systems. SIEM tools also facilitate audit record correlation and analysis.

SIEM technology utilizes known correlation of events and mathematical algorithms to provide real-time analysis of security alerts and/or potential threats generated via network and security devices, identity management applications, vulnerability management tools, as well as operating system, application system, and database management system logs.

SIEM tools proactively monitor events in real-time to identify attacks as they are happening as opposed to discovering and responding to attacks that may not be discovered for days or weeks after an event.

System Hardening and Configuration Management

At this time, there are no formalized procedures or baselines for configuring and hardening systems and devices on COMPANY networks. The configurations of servers, workstations, Apple Devices and other similar devices typically exist as disk images. The various configurations should be documented and updated on a continual basis. The disk images should consistently be scanned with a vulnerability scanner and tested to determine if there are any vulnerabilities that should be remediated or mitigated. Disk images for servers, workstations, Apple Devices, and other devices should be subjected to stringent change control and any changes should be documented and tested. It is important to apply OS updates and patches to keep the images up to date as the images will be used to configure new servers, workstations, or other devices across COMPANY networks when needed.

NIST SP 800-123 is the guideline for General Server Security. The theme of the guideline is that "Organizations should carefully plan and address the security aspects of the deployment of a server." Hardening a server involves configuring the server's OS, Basic Input Output System (BIOS), and applications hosted on the server to ensure the system is as secure as possible before placing the system in the production environment.

Most vendors advocate a defense-in-depth approach to harden their products that may include changing the physical hardware configuration, changing the BIOS settings, and making additional changes regarding the principle of least-use, object authorization, disabling unnecessary services, and enabling audit trail features. Some vendors provide an automated hardening process while others provide a checklist contained within a document, such as a "read me" file that comes with the system.

The Center for Internet Security (CIS) is an excellent source for security benchmark information. According to the CIS website, "The CIS Security Benchmarks program is recognized as a trusted, independent authority that facilitates the collaboration of public and private industry experts to achieve consensus on practical and actionable solutions."

The following CIS Security Benchmarks program resources are available for download at no cost:

- Operating Systems
- Database Servers
- Network Devices
- Web Browsers
- Mobile Devices
- Virtualization

In addition to the security benchmarks, CIS also offers a free tool, the CIS-Configuration Assessment Tool (CAT) which is a Java-based tool that compares the configuration of target IT systems to CIS Benchmarks and reports conformance scores on a scale of 0-100. CIS-CAT is listed on the NVD website as a SCAP-validated authenticated configuration scanner.

Because the benchmarks could fill the role of missing security configuration standards and the assessment tool could report conformance to the benchmarks, OCS has expressed their desire to use the CIS Security Benchmarks and CIS-CAT to the maximum degree possible.

Basic Input Output System (BIOS)

The Basic Input Output System (BIOS) is the lowest level of software/firmware defining system configuration and low-level hardware. Typically, BIOS is configured to prevent attackers from being able to reboot the computer to manipulate the system for malicious purposes.

BIOS hardening is done in accordance with vendor provided instructions.

Impact of Security Controls

Controls are a means of assuring a process operates in the intended way. For information security processes, security controls are used to mitigate the risk of an attack being successful which could result in the compromise of Restricted Information. There are several different types of security controls. Controls can be preventive in nature or they can be detective. Controls can also be corrective or compensatory. Controls can be automated or they can be manual. Some controls are implemented to mitigate the risk of certain threats, or threat agents, exploiting certain vulnerabilities.

To visualize the critical impact of security controls, various elements that would be incorporated to analyze various IT threat profiles, IT asset components along with associated threats, threat agents, vulnerability exploits and the resulting consequences have been mapped to the supporting security controls in Table 5 below.

Table 5. IT Asset Component Threat Profiles Mapped to Security Controls

Component		Threat	Threat Agent	Vulnerability		Security Controls
				Exploit	Consequence	
Software	Operating System (Windows, Unix)	Adversary	Malware	Lack of anti-virus/malware SW	Infected system	Encryption, Vulnerability Scans, Penetration Testing File Integrity Monitoring, Log Monitoring (SIEM), Patch Management, System Hardening Malware Protection
		Adversary	User, Hacker, Cracker	Misconfigured system	System malfunction	
				Illegal privilege escalation	Unauthorized access to Restricted Data	
					System malfunction	
	General-Purpose application (browser, SQL)	Adversary	User, Hacker, Cracker	Misconfigured system	System malfunction	Encryption, Web-App Firewall (WAF), Web-App Pen-Testing, Secure Coding Testing & QA, SDLC Controls, Role Based Access and Least Privilege ACL & Firewall Rules
	System-Specific Application (Care Connect)				Unauthorized access to Restricted Information	
	Web-Applications	Adversary	Hacker, Cracker	Poorly written application	Creating a buffer overflow	

Component		Threat	Threat	Vulnerability		Security Controls
				Poor adherence to best practices	Unauthorized access to Restricted Information	
				Invalid firewall or ACL settings		
Hardware	Networking Equipment (router, switch, IDS/IPS, etc.)	Adversary	Hacker, Cracker	Misconfigured system	Unauthorized access to Restricted Information	Encryption, Network Intrusion Detection and Prevention (IDS/IPS), Log Monitoring (SIEM) System Hardening, Configuration Management, External Penetration Testing, Internal Network Scanning ACL & Firewall Rules
				Invalid firewall or ACL settings		
	Duplication (copiers, printers, multifunction, VOIP Phones, VTC)	User	User	User Error	Accidental disclosure of Restricted Information	
				Invalid firewall or ACL settings	Unauthorized access to Restricted Information	
Personnel		Personnel	Employees	Lack of auditing	Altering Restricted Information	Train Personnel, Documentation Review, Audit Review, Role Based Access (RBAC) Privileged Access Controls Password Controls Log Monitoring (SIEM) Data Loss Prevention (DLP)
					Privilege escalation	
				Lack of training or policy enforcement	Theft of Restricted Information	
			Contractors	Lack of access control safeguards		

Revision History

Rev.	Responsible	Description of Revision	Release Date

APPENDIX A: REFERENCES

References used in this document are listed below.

1. Center for Internet Security, Critical Security Controls V5.1

2. Center for Internet Security, Security Benchmarks Program and Configuration Assessment Tool (CAT)

3. Centers for Medicare and Medicaid Services, Office of Civil Rights, Guidance on Risk Analysis Requirements under the HIPAA Security Rule, Posted July 14, 2010

4. Information System Audit and Control Association, Control Objectives for Information and Related Technology 5, 2012

5. International Organization for Standardization/International Electro technical Commission (ISO/IEC) 27001, Information technology -- Security techniques -- Information security management systems – Requirements, 2013

6. International Organization for Standardization/International Electro technical Commission (ISO/IEC) 27002, Information technology — Security techniques — Code of practice for information security controls, 2013

7. National Institute of Standards and Technology Special Publication 800-40, Revision 3, Guide to Enterprise Patch Management Technologies, July 2013

8. National Institute of Standards and Technology Special Publication 800-53, Revision 4, Recommended Security Controls for Federal Information Systems and Organizations, April 2013

9. National Institute of Standards and Technology Special Publication 800-64, Revision 2, Security Considerations in the System Development Life Cycle, October 2008

10. National Institute of Standards and Technology Special Publication 800-66, Revision 1, An Introductory Resource Guide for Implementing the Health Insurance Portability and Accountability Act (HIPAA) Security Rule, October 2008

11. National Institute of Standards and Technology Special Publication 800-115, Technical Guide to Information Security Testing and Assessment, September 2008

12. National Institute of Standards and Technology Special Publication 800-123, Guide to General Server Security, July 2008

13. National Institute of Standards and Technology Interagency Reports 7298, Revision 2, Glossary of Key Information Security Terms, May 2013

14. System Administration, Audit, Network, and Security Information Security Reading Room, Implementing a Vulnerability Management Process

15. U.S Department of Energy, Office of Electricity Delivery and Energy Reliability, Cybersecurity Capability Maturity Model Version 1.1, February 2014

APPENDIX B: GLOSSARY

COMMON TERMS AND DEFINITIONS

*nix	An operating system that behaves in a manner similar to that of a UNIX operating system without necessarily conforming to the Single UNIX Specification family of standards to be called Unix .
Access Control List	Most network security systems operate by allowing selective use of services. An access control list is the usual means by which access to, and denial of, services are controlled. It is simply a list of the services available, each with a list of the hosts permitted to use the service.
Authorized Individual	A University employee, student, contractor, or other individual affiliated with the University who has been granted authorization by a Resource Proprietor, or his or her designee, to access a Resource and who invokes or accesses a Resource for the purpose of performing his or her job duties or other functions directly related to his or her affiliation with the University. The authorization granted is for a specific level of access to a Resource as designated by the Resource Proprietor, unless otherwise defined by University policy.
Availability	The property that data or information is accessible and useable upon demand by an authorized person.
Confidentiality	The property that data or information is not made available or disclosed to unauthorized persons or processes.
Cracker	A cracker is an individual who attempts to access computer systems without authorization. These individuals are often malicious, as opposed to hackers, and have many means at their disposal for breaking into a system.
Demilitarized Zone	A physical or logical subnetwork (sometimes referred to as a perimeter network) that contains and exposes an organization's external-facing services to a larger and untrusted network, usually the Internet. The purpose of a DMZ is to add an additional layer of security to an organization's local area network. External users only have direct access to equipment in the DMZ, rather than any other part of the internal network.
Device	A computer, printer, wireless appliance, or other piece of equipment that can connect to and communicate over any COMPANY network. Devices would include, but are not limited to, workstations, Apple Devices, laptops, notebooks, tablets, application servers, web servers, database servers, and medical and other devices with network connectivity.

Threat and Vulnerability Management Program

Essential Resource	A resource is designated as Essential if its failure to function correctly and on schedule could result in (1) a major failure by a Campus to perform mission-critical functions, (2) a significant loss of funds or information, or (3) a significant liability or other legal exposure to a Campus.
Hacker	A person who delights in having an intimate understanding of the internal workings of a system, computers and computer networks in particular. The term is often misused in a pejorative context, where "cracker" would be the correct term.
Hotfix	Microsoft's term for a security patch
Integrity	The property that data or information have not been altered or destroyed in an unauthorized manner.
Malware	"Malware" is short for malicious software and used as a single term to refer to virus, spy ware, worm etc. Malware is designed to cause damage to a stand-alone computer or a networked workstation including Apple Devices. So wherever a malware term is used it means a program which is designed to damage your computer it may be a virus, worm or Trojan.
MedNet	The data network connecting COMPANY Health Medical Centers, the COMPANY Health Faculty Practice Group, and the David Geffen School of Medicine.
Mitigation	Applying one or more controls or safeguards to reduce the likelihood of an unwanted occurrence and/or lessen its consequences.
Office of Civil Rights	A component of the Centers for Medicare and Medicaid Services, the Office of Civil Rights is responsible for enforcing the HIPAA Privacy and Security Rules (45 C.F.R. Parts 160 and 164, Subparts A, C, and E).
Patch	An additional piece of code developed to address a problem in an existing piece of software.
Plan of Action	A Plan of Action and Milestones, also referred to as a Remediation Plan, is a management tool outlining identified information security program and system weaknesses along with the tasks necessary to mitigate them. To facilitate the remediation of weaknesses, the Plan of Actions and Milestones process provides a means of planning and monitoring corrective actions; defines roles and responsibilities for solving problems; assists in identifying security funding requirements; tracks and prioritizes resources; and informs decision-makers.
Remediation	The act of correcting a vulnerability, or multiple vulnerabilities, or eliminating a threat. Some possible types of remediation are: installing a patch, adjusting configuration settings, terminating processes running on a server, and uninstalling a software application.

Resource Custodian	The individual(s) who have physical or logical control over Electronic Information Resources. This role provides a service to the Resource Proprietor.
Resource Proprietor	The individual(s) designated responsibility for the information and the processes supporting the University function. Resource Proprietors are responsible for ensuring compliance with federal or state law or regulation or University policy regarding the release of information according to procedures established by the University, the campus, or the department, as applicable to the situation. All Electronic Information Resources are University resources, and Resource Proprietors are responsible for ensuring that these Resources are used in ways consistent with the mission of the University as a whole.
Resource Providers	Organizational units with operational responsibility to provide and manage electronic information services used to conduct University business by Authorized Individuals, such as financial or student information systems. These resources are generally network-based, but may not necessarily be so.
Restricted Information	Restricted information describes any confidential or personal information protected by law or policy which requires the highest level of access control and security protection, whether in storage or in transit. Typically, Restricted Information most often refers to ePHI covered by the HIPAA Security Rule. The term "restricted" should not be confused with that used by the University of California managed national laboratories where federal programs may employ a different classification scheme.
Threat	Any circumstance or event, deliberate or unintentional, with the potential for causing harm to a system.
Threat Agent	An entity with the potential to exploit a vulnerability, or multiple vulnerabilities.
Trojan Horse	A computer program which carries within itself a means to allow the creator of the program access to the system using it.
Virus	A program which replicates itself on computer systems by incorporating itself into other programs which are shared among computer systems.
Windows Server Update Services	Enables information technology administrators to deploy the latest Microsoft product updates to computers that are running the Windows operating system. By using this tool, administrators can fully manage the distribution of updates that are released through Microsoft Update to computers in their network.
Worm	A computer program which replicates itself and is self-propagating. Worms, as opposed to viruses, are meant to spawn in network environments.
Zero-Day Attack	A zero-day attack, or vulnerability, refers to a software vulnerability that is unknown to the vendor. The vulnerability is then exploited by hackers before the vendor

becomes aware of it and hurries to fix it—this exploit is typically called a zero-day attack

APPENDIX C ACRONYMS

Acronyms used in this document are listed below

3DES	Triple DES
ACL	Access Control List
AES	Advanced Encryption Standard
APT	Advanced Persistent Threat
AV	Anti-Virus
BA	Business Associates
BFB	Business and Finance Bulletin
BIOS	Basic Input Output System
CAT	Configuration Assessment Tool
C2M2	Cybersecurity Capability Maturity Model
CCEP	Common Configuration Enumeration Project
CDE	Cardholder Data Environment
CIS	Center for Internet Security
CMS	Centers for Medicare and Medicaid Services
CSC	Computer Support Coordinator
CSIRT	Computer Security Incident Response Team
CVE	Common Vulnerabilities and Exposures
CVSS	Common Vulnerability Scoring System
DES	Data Encryption Standard
DISA	Defense Information Systems Agency
DLP	Data Loss Prevention
DMZ	Demilitarized Zone
ePHI	Electronic Protected Health Information
FDE	Full Disk Encryption
FIM	File Integrity Monitoring
FIRST	Forum of Incident Response and Security Teams
FPG	Faculty Practice Group
FTP	File Transfer Protocol
HIDS	Host Intrusion Detection System

HIPAA	Health Insurance Portability and Accountability Act
HIPS	Host Intrusion Prevention System
HSECOB	Health Sciences Enterprise Compliance Oversight Board
HSSC	Security Committee
HTTP	Hypertext Transfer Protocol
HTTPS	Hypertext Transfer Protocol Secure
ICS-CERT	Industrial Control Systems Cyber Emergency Response Team
IDS	Intrusion Detection System
IEC	International Electrotechnical Committee
IP	Internet Protocol
IPS	Intrusion Prevention System
IR	Interagency Report
IS	Information System or Information Security
ISAC	Information Sharing and Analysis Center
ISACA	Information System Audit and Control Association
ISO	International Organization for Standardization
IS	Information Services and Solutions
ISTR	Internet Security Threat Report (Symantec)
IT	Information Technology
ITAM	IT Asset Management
MedNet	Medical Network
MIL	Maturity Indicator Level
MITM	Man-In-The-Middle
MITS	Medical Information Technology Services
NSA	National Security Agency
NIST	National Institute of Standards and Technology
Nmap	Network Mapper

NVD   National Vulnerability Database

OCR   Office of Civil Rights

OCS   Office of Compliance Services

OS   Operating System

OSI   Open Systems Interconnection

OT   Operational Technology

OWASP Open Web Application Security Project

PHI   Protected Health Information

PII   Personally Identifiable Information

QA   Quality Assurance

RBAC   Role Based Access Control

SANS   System Administration, Audit, Network, and Security

SCAP   Security Content Automation Protocol

SCG   Security Configuration Guide

SDLC   Software Development Life Cycle

SFTP   SSH File Transfer Protocol

SIEM   Security Information and Event Management

SLA   Service Level Agreement

SME   Subject Matter Expert

SOMITS School of Medicine Information Technology Services

SOP   Standard Operating Procedure

SP   Special Publication

SSH   Secure Shell

SSL   Secure Sockets Layer

SSN   Social Security Number

SQL   Structured Query Language

STIG   Security Technical Implementation Guide

TCP   Transport Control Protocol

TDEA   Triple Data Encryption Algorithm

TLS   Transport Layer Security

TVM   Threat and vulnerability management

US-CERT United States Computer Emergency Response Team

VoIP   Voice over Internet Protocol

VTC   Video Teleconference

WAF   Web Application Firewall

WSUS   Windows Server Updates Services

XSS   Cross-Site Scripting